DELIVERED

Also by Sarah Gambito

Matadora

A KAREN & MICHAEL BRAZILLER BOOK
PERSEA BOOKS / NEW YORK

POEMS

DELIVERED
SARAH GAMBITO

Persea Books, Inc.
853 Broadway
New York, NY 10003

Printed in the U.S.A.
Designed by Bookrest.
First edition.

Library of Congress Cataloging-in-Publication Data

Gambito, Sarah Verdes.

    Delivered : poems / Sarah Gambito. -- 1st ed.
    p. cm.
    "A Karen & Michael Braziller book."
    ISBN 978-0-89255-346-4 (trade pbk. : alk. paper)
    1. Filipino American women--Poetry. I. Title.
    PS3607.A433D45 2009
    811'.6--dc22
                               2008031269

Acknowledgments

Grateful acknowledgment goes to the following publications, in which some of these poems first appeared: *Barrow Street, Denver Quarterly, Fence, Field, Indiana Review, jubilat, OCHO* and *Shampoo*.

To Joseph O. Legaspi—My true blue heart-sender.

Thank you, Gabriel Fried, for believing.

Opals to Rebecca, Carlito, Christine, Steve, Micah, Pavneet Singh, Tan Lin, Kron Vollmer, Charlotte Meehan, Jennifer Chang, Aaron Baker, Eddie del Rosario, Jimmy Yan, Marilyn Rifkin, Rita Zilberman, Suki Kim, Oliver de la Paz, Vikas Menon, Matt Paco, Aimee Nezhukumatathil, Patrick Rosal, David Mura, Jon Pineda, Heather Bryant, Marilyn Chin, Saladin Ahmed, Marlon Esguerra, Bino Realuyo, Leah Melycher, Prageeta Sharma, Arthur Sze, Edward Bok Lee, Kimiko Hahn, Jennifer Presant, James Kim, Cecily Parks, Raymond de Leon, Major Jackson, Catalino Eusebio, Marie Sarmiento, Carolyn Micklem, Cornelius Eady, Toi Derricote, Mei-mei Berssenbrugge, and Jennifer Lee.

And I give thanks to my family, the same: Kundiman.

I am indebted also to The MacDowell Colony and The New York Foundation for the Arts.

Contents

[BABY COYOTE]

I.

He took me; He drew me out of many waters.
He brought me forth also into a spacious place;
He delivered me, because He **delighted in me.**

—*Psalm 18:16,19*

Immigration

So what if I don't love you.
My problems don't even happen to me.

But to three girls grandstanding by the Potomac.
Respectively: your mother, her mother and her mother.
Three bitches in front of a trashcan.
Desirous of psychotherapy and a split lip courtesy of me.
Because I didn't ask to be born here.
Didn't ask to learn the language.
And don't know how to save you.

Am I frightening you?
I'm frightening you.

Good and good and good and good.

Toro

I'm looking for the good robin of everlasting sewing.

Easy as a bed to bed.

And his words are mints.

My shock in the ghost of the guest of my boyfriend.

First there is the Father.

He would not like me to tell you about him.

He is punching holes right now. Saying petit, petit, petit.

Garbled—he can seem like a balloon. Such a skin. A kingfisher.

We are afraid to touch him.

Like too many nights of touching ourselves.

He might plan to take us on a picnic.

We must be ready. We must be hungry.

I finished my blue necklace.

She tries to convince him because he was here on earth.

Dad quits his job for the umpteenth time.

I'm wicked lonely.

We are in a department store.

I buy him a blue bracelet because it is right there.

And I would wear it.

I buy it hoping he bought me something for Christmas.

This is never true of course.

We talk about religion. Of jasper things in trees.

He wears an engagement ring.

I am shivery, full of V-8.

He drinks too much and cheats all the time.

All of whom he left behind in the Bible belt are singing *Yes, yes, yes.*

We put our hands over our face, our neck.

We are overcome saying "No, no. I can't. I can't."

For My Attention

I opened a melon last night and immigrants spilled out of it.
Careless and eager. They bit me for my attention.

My mother wore a red suit because she loved her job.
She spoke with italics sprinkled in. A mouthy sequin. Only for her.
And so she could share with me.
Tell me stories about paris. Debonair painters who love her.

That I could hold myself like a good melon.
Bright and eager with stories and beautiful painters who are my friends.

I believed that god could rest with me. Like a white tired dove
of david copperfield's blond women.
She would rest on the wet shoulder of my pillow.

Your voice can startle you.
"I'd have visited sooner."
An appetite. A fish.
Its scales scare it.
Its habitat scares it.

I've been pretending to be fine with it all.
As in like *nothing*.
To feel the eely middle of the moment.

Holding the umbilical cord in one hand
and a pair of diamondback shears in the other.
This ice-defying birth that I've engineered.
One fear after another.

Take your hands out of the icky painting and say
place your hands on her head like so.
And bless me.

Repository of your own octane rest. Bless me for vitamins.
More teething for the biting. All the better to bite you
with my licorice lickitysplit concourse.
Bleeding down the superdome.

Immigration

The death of the grain and the death of the god are one and the same.
The resurrection of the grain and the resurrection of the god are one and the same.

—*The Book of the Dead*

Quick to the cut I dream about grass growing next to each other.
One screaming the other screaming back until it changes species.
= what I'm capable of.

As could happen. But not definitely.
Whodunit, who's whistling?

It's my "race" I say.
And I'm so exhausted.

Visitor's parlance. Sheer as in "able to."
Mahal ko, bakit hindi ka maka tulog.

And then, I'm guessing again.
Looking at myself like a Labrador.

I want to ignore something so much it becomes quieter than me.

The vampire is an initiator par excellence.
Inside the hand strokes and strokes.
Obviously the hand needs no approval.
The hand says, "You will."

These are not always horror films. But she will.
She rises and bites her.

I wanted to reach China when I was a girl.
I dug until my hands were spirits. Free in me.
Grilled to perfection. Ancien regime.

I am the new bathing suit that I am.
Dewy, doggy boulevard.

Every Khu, an aspect of the soul,
seeking admission to paradise was referred to an Osiris.
As passageway. As *more* than dead.

Love in love's seed pod
analogous to itself.

It wants to grow arms. Be a big boy.
Give me gingham presents.

Be here now. Be better.

The Puppy

Immigrant families began to arrive and children were born. Eventually
the children picked up English at school. The English was cool and light
like a puppy but more useful. They picked it up and threw it at each other
at playgrounds. Some were better than others. Some just thought it
was cute but a waste of time. Some compared back legs and the length
of fur and the set of the nose and the wide dripping eyes. Even if they
didn't say so everyone competed.

I need you to understand

—After Emmanuel Ghent

The thrust of this poem is not to challenge or discredit the vast literature
on masochism and the ever sharpening insight into its psychic functions
and meanings, but to attempt to illumine the shroud of mystery that still
hangs over this curious human phenomenon—the seeking out of
submission, pain or adversity for the purpose of acquiring states of
"home." Meaning I'm melty. I'm succulence through and through. Or
I'm just "through." Get off the property. Both states demand action.
And, if one is lucky, beach chairs. To determine which action is implied
requires a level of faith few are capable of. By faith, I mean to point to
a way of experiencing which is undertaken with one's whole being, all
out, with one's heart, with one's soul and with all one's might. Forgetting
everything in the original country.

Because I'm Supposed To

Egrets on the rim of how you love me.
How your love is a feather, feathers under my head.
That leaves over my body. And leaves in fall. Leaves that people see.

I need your friends so much.

Because you love me and your friends
with all the pliers try another relationship.
I'm wearing something that says Your Present. And I cry.

How does a family begin? How not to take its loop.
The small leather bound volumes glinting
along the threshed bone of me with my dress shucked earlier.

Still, I cared for him as he ladled the leafy vegetables onto my plate.
We're together in this quizzling, quivering thresh of light.

Hunger

I had a canoe that took me into the forest I read about. It was fleet and I asked no questions. I saw the careless embroidery of the sky above me. I was small. I was embracing. And I was dear all my life. My instrument is silent. I never learned to play. But it sits poised in my arms like an amber deer that I'll give my life for. What does it sound like? Why haven't I tried?

She crept into my arms like a red flower a stranger gives me. She is tame and soft. In a low voice, I tell her stories of when I was a girl. I bring her fruit from the brook of my own glad tidings. I overflow and I almost forget her. My hair is wet and I feel I can be alone. I know other songs. But what about my deer? She's sleeping. I fit an arrow through my bow. I kill so she eats. She says if only I'd been a better mother.

Ethnicity is a Noodle King

A long gamble through the subway. Location

we don't propose only deem estimable.

I am devoted to that which does not make me distinct.

Race as to be written of forcefully, from within the gut, from within the flaw.

Today our students (who, even now, study race) are achingly familiar.

They make mistakes but wear radiant nightgowns.

How to pick one out?

This is the one I need most—

or as much as the others.

It is my hope that she needs me back.

The Puppy

I was talking to a couple about attachment theory. And their little girl was so sweet. They said do you remember it. And I couldn't remember. They just held their baby. Everyone was suckling. It was a darling. It made me puppyish and wanting to jump on people. Mom had given me all these crusty bakery goods which I was proud of and ashamed of at once. I said this can't happen again. What if I get pregnant. I don't want to talk to you for a while. I'll call if I'm pregnant. Ok. So we can go through the dismissal process together. I was ashamed because she was so sweet and I had no real memory of her.

I didn't know everyone else could do this

I was in trouble. Able to bring in a cold wind and announce my decisions and my type of mood to the world. And everything all at once was filled with a strong wind.

Burning the lamp of the loving hunter, I was lonely and it could crush my immediate surroundings. I didn't warn anyone because I wanted them to join me. I hoped we could remark together. Feet flat on an amiable countryside. Blooms extending. The white heart of belief plunging down into America.

I drew languorous ghosts in my room. My eye was sharp and companies would check me out. The ghosts wanted butter and sublime cuts of meat. I couldn't keep up. My fingers were caught. I sucked on blood and became strong.

With so much fruit, the cellars were confused. I didn't want to be associated. I went to exhibitions and cried aloud for the paleontologist's renderings. The little girl's feet. They were radioactive and I was young. I spent so much money. Luckily, I didn't have anyone else to think of.

II.

Migrants worldwide sent home an estimated **$300 billion** last year—nearly three times the world's foreign-aid budgets combined. These sums—"remittances"—bring Morocco more money than tourism does. They bring Sri Lanka more money than tea does.

—The New York Times Magazine, April 22, 2007

The Good Provider

The best thing of all is to take the enemy's country whole and intact.
My mother took my heart out. She banked it on top of her stove.
It glowed white. She put it back in my chest.

Tita knew that overseas workers often had affairs.
He licked me and I pretended it pinged through my body like a swift idea
That I wrote about and considered like a bell of good craftsmanship.
She also knew that their kids ate better

He said your belly is like a cat's.
He said with his bowl up to his chin
More please.

At night the fireflies come out. They flock to my window.
I put my hands up against the screen.
I think how fragile it is to be inside a house.
They say I want permission

I paint my face. I say—just take it.
Easy. If equally matched, we can offer battle.
If unequal in any way, we can flee from him.

Deprived of their father while sustained by his wages.
I thought a lot about walking around at night.
By myself. Just to think. But I never did.
I thought I could just flick a switch.

When I was born, my mother and father gave me a gardenia like personal star.
Don't you hate it when someone apologizes all the time?
It's like they are not even sorry.

Reasonable Evidence

I said, aside from your beauty

       what do people in a room notice about you?

She said Depends *what room*.

       I ordered a gimlet.

I ordered *gin*.

       I said yes because I didn't understand

and I hoped they were agreeing with me.

       Yes to the youngest sister.

These bright penny citizens.

       Crawling fixedly over internal laws

Because I can't enjoy it.

       Throwing all the blue medicine beautiful bottles

Off the sick everything.

       You were the smarter canon that saw through it all.

And was a santa anna.

        You were born here. I was born there.

And as you had no harlequin,

        We were a family, a jailbird of unequal delights.

Waiting

Salvacion changing her name to Ashley. No Ashlee she says.

 (Accent on the ee)

What keeps me filipino? Loving stinky fish?

When the ship was pulling away. I was dying on his lapels.

I was hoping I was the girl I was.

I am not every grain of wheat. Although I'd like to be

Spread out like a carpet of talkative nodding kindnesses.

Surely I'm not interchangeable?

What if I really don't recognize you.

This is why I don't like your flowers.

Able to exit so languidly. By proxy.

I can't take anything flowershape leaving me.

Even you dear reader. Stay again.

Let me try again.

Thirst

When God was a cup of coffee,
I laid my mouth down
to begin the day ordinarily.
The girl inside the girl.
Grown all manly and lover-like.

I catch myself like a dove.
Just 15 minutes ago.

The whole kernel flies up and hits the sky with shout.
Myself broken apart in several rubies.

And I am afraid it can't happen again.
That even the book is too much.

One then two.
Two then one.

My father says Bibigay ang Diyos isang Peking Duck or two?
Is God going to give us one Peking Duck or two?

My lover has never had Peking duck.
He does not look disposed.

I like God alright but I don't understand anything he's talking about.
There he is blinking beside the ferris wheel.

On the ferris wheel, her God-book flew out of her lap and she was relieved.
She screamed you bitch. Try to see where it lands.
Try to feel my thoughts for it.

Two Times

I dreamed that everyone forgot my birthday and even Loralei was insulting. She said we did mary lou retton and everyone liked it. And your impression just wasn't that successful. Mom wanted to have a party after church. We were going to eat Chef Boyardee and I was thinking of making a fancier cream pasta. After closing hymn, there were announcements. Mom was asking me if we should announce my party. And I said no. She asked me two times I said no two times—secretly not wanting to spend my time with all these church people I didn't know. Then mom said that she couldn't do it. Anyway. And so there wasn't even the celebration that I didn't want.

Durian Fruit is Sweet

But wards off even the most angling tourist

with its bitchy smell.

Identifying with its aggressor

I am the threat.

Inside the solider. Like inside the anime.

It's easier when I can hold it.

Alopecia Example.

You can cross the perimeter if

the genitalia are yours. Cavalcade

forward on simple pencil strokes.

That's me doing just fine.

Squeezing the unreal, unfilled representative.

I in wrinkled dress and quaking sandwich.

Waving octopi home. Resilient.

Non-communicative. Just arms all the time.

All around.

A Borderless Ethos Would Please Everyone

This is what makes everyone naturally American.

They want to wind up their American.

Who can blame them.

Access to reliable birth control.

Meeting strangers over the Internet.

Your American is a little late.

He was eating pizza and forgot the time.

He buys drinks.

My American is polite and buys drinks back for you.

It continues like this.

I write with my dogs

So they don't observe the creepy crawlies of their doubts shimmering
in the background. I write because I'm pack leader. I want them to stay
the course. Whether it's for water or better boyfriends. My will is theirs.

It's important that I know our old grievance. That I slide down on the
bathroom floor in front of our original country. There was a map on his
wall with everything pinned to where he had been. I felt each location.
I listened with every ear I had. I slid to the floor. I said this is where we
are going to go.

One Minute

What would it do to curse you
in my learned languages.
To curse the left leg with the right.

Semper Fi.
Il pleure dans mon coeur

Panicking and picnicking
With yourself and a bad shovel.
Breaking into amethysts
sighing at last.

A Borderless Ethos Would Please Everyone

I

But everyone says I just want to look.

I won't touch.

On TV I watch you drive grand armed cars.

I imagine the lush seats as an expensive, brushy wine I can't name.

But who I'd like to share with a girl: Carla, Racine, Maria.

A peppery jolting effect.

Look, no hands!

I saw her movie.

Braids brushing the blinking explorer's face.

She was brown and graceful.

Like a land she danced on.

She said I'm yours.

And I wanted her to say that to me too.

II

But then what happens to my fringe element boy poems?

Picking at vermin in their hair.

And always something tenuous to say.

To be built for the office. Cracking jokes and hanging

onto the color printer for life.

A café. A cordial. A cordial partner. Cordials & a partner.

I wish I could pull it off and wail into the badge.

III

Let's make it more specific.

If I stood next to my grandmother,

headless secrets with droplets of water not here

But over there would condense on my new clothes.

I would be alluring to myself.

I'd lick my arm.

I'd tell her an obvious joke.

One she can see running toward her like a frantic, clean-shaven father.

IV

I'm scared

It won't heal anything.

It will heal your foot.

She could ejaculate all over her coach.

And he wanted me to do that too.

Don't you kiiyaaaaaa?

Kiiiayyyaaa!

Kiiiayyyaaa.

Because I'm sick of pretending that everything is a brierpatch hymnal.

Or that I'm close to them.

Close to you close to myself how do I get closer.

I say like a new, chewing boyfriend to myself.

You let it go a little.

You don't need everything to be a gymnast.

Relying on herself. All the livelongday.

V

Help me to sit at the feet of this lettuce defense.

I've become so hungry that I'm the default reason.

Give me its jawbone.

I'll kill its honey-lion.

I'm stronger than our own protection.

Reserved and ever patient.

I sprang to my defense.

I was better than you.

I wanted it more.

VI

I look at the save the children ads.

I am young and lambent.

They can't wipe the rubbery flies off their face.

Big eyes and convulsive smiles.

I said *We have to do something to help her.*

They laughed and said that it was just TV.

But I cram the photographs in her face.

It's the united states and can't she wake up.

I say was it like this.

VII

I'm not making it up.

Jamming four fingers into a dead toy.

I felt like I wanted to tell him.

Sundry, elevator, striped, searching things.

I was born after the world wars.

I can't touch your hands.

Let me. Give me.

My church's silky, sad hair.

Rosa

Rosa is an immigrant to the U.S.
Rosa is an émigré from the Philippines.

Rosa immigrates her favorite plant.
The Favorite Plant emigrates two coyote wails for water.

Like this *Haaaa, haaaa.*

Rosa immigrates West and discovers coffee colored shoes.
I emigrate East and discover the same shoes.
We are surprised and angry at the same party.

I discover rosa but I'm not too excited about it.
I've seen these weedy things over and over again.

Please don't discover me says Rosa her arms full of glistering rosas.
I say, of course. I say, I knew it. I pedal-to-the-metal it.

Rosa

Tired, rose-blown, rose-centered and putting roses on a card for you.
Thinking from your vantage point, "How will you see these roses?" Will
you see what I can't write down. Calliope and running after yourself.
The yellow lines of subtitles scrolling by in another language. When I
laugh, it's in another language. And for deliciousness sake, I gasp in
another language. Arrange to meet you by metro stops. Risk adverse.
My handwriting careful and pulling bad doves from the air and placing
them on her shoulder. I'm vulnerable and fire ready. Staying too
long at the dance. Watching them grilling fish by the beach. Where
will they think of next? Will they actually go? Will they miss me? I'm
adventurous I tell myself.

Bedtime

If I touch red-riding-hood, she screeches and I am flummoxed

and ready to hit her if I see her again.

Sometimes I think the words and daughters are sugar cubes

that will melt away in front of any danger.

I tell the daughter in a turtleneck—how dare you.

I pick her up and pick her up at school. I have to and we resent it..

The daughter grows two limpid horns of learning.

She shuffles and is an alto singer.

Her horns as spry as an onion. Commonplace and fragrant.

A something sizzling on purpose.

To come home to something sustenance.

It hurts when you touch it like that.

Touch it again.

I like seeing a clean reflex.

It can't help itself.

And is never guilty.

The university loves the daughter. They hold hands

and create clubs and ginseng, other assorted remedies for la grippe.

Who's more impatient. Who's better than you.

I huddle with you. We say to each other

I wish I could be like you.

I had a dream

Just you with a dream like a farm tool in your mouth. And when you speak of systems of gathering and leaving. The poorer women would follow after and gather the left pieces of grain.

Ruth said to Boaz your god is my god. I will follow you (or was that to Naomi) but they fell in love. "Falling into delicious snow."

I woke up in a panic. Thinking I was in Manila and I didn't have a choice and I lived in Manila and Manila was my address and that's what happened to me.

Someone was singing no woman no cry. What did we know of women. Of a woman crying. Of me. As a woman crying. But to want to be where you are. To feel the museum chilling through your body.

What is blue to blueviolet? That I need you across this terrible divide. I need an experience of myself as it grows older. Less remembered. More agile. Taking on its own hazel eyes. Assigning themselves to different parts of my body, my family. You were the one who was left you. Were the one who left.

Fear of Natural Enemies

Avoid animals that seem to be behaving abnormally.
Especially wild animals that seem too friendly.

Not even a dog.
If I could bite it.

Janie looks in at her soul.
As if I can bite it.

The women spread the food out.
We oil it, pat it, poke it, shred it, boil it, mince it,
fry it, bake it, season it, marinate it.

I want to feel sex.
And you cringe from me as I gain power.

God recreates in the cool of the evening.
with rusty bayonet and the look of an untender professor.

Janie looks in at her soul.

What if it was just an accident.
In the cool of the evening,

He happens upon man and woman and converses with them.
I'm won't die in an office cubicle, not in the arms of a frightening novelist.

We admire curly, indigo plants. She says, "Let's touch the lily."
I'm in the belly of the beast. If I am me. I. Hack my way out.

And, it hurts like a big dog.
Janie looks in at her soul.

My last relative.
Crazy with her cellophane bags of jewelry.

Says no it was "force." It was "force."
My fronds.

I picked her up. Her provisions.
And, by accident, dropped her

What came out was so much ketchup.
Fake and fake.

I'd like to meet someone Janie says.

Someone who doesn't make me want
to hit him over the head with barbecue tongs.

Janie looks in at her soul.

My soul is a brutal logger having known no fine porridge or satiny
ornaments. My soul gestures strongly to the waterfalls up ahead. And
forces barges and dreamboats towards the squalling musk of urbane
normalcy. My soul grunts. My soul hugs himself at night. My soul
practices to itself in private.

Oh truculent, oh leafy, oh crouching evergiving.

What if it was just an accident?
Janie looks in at her soul.

Bite because angry? Bite because scared?
Bite because confused?

An infected dog may viciously attack any moving object, person, or animal.
A caged rabid dog will chew the wire and break her teeth.

III.

I sometimes wake up in the middle of the night
with a hole in my chest
lava running down my eyes
the sheets all covered with blood
my inner radio playing a scratchy bolero
I wake up alone
within the....emptiness of America....
I begin to cry like a **baby coyote**
I long for the garden of my childhood
& the blatant affection of my relatives & neighbors
who always forgave my excesses and contradictions.

—*Guillermo Gómez-Peña, Warrior for Gringostoika*

If there is a Poem within this Poem

She wants to sleep in your arms.

It's her birthday.

And bright cake lulls in your stomach.

Let's begin again.

Name two rights of everyone living in the U.S.

(Hint choose any of the below.
See I told you I'd help you.)

> Freedom of expression
> Freedom of speech
> Freedom of assembly
> Freedom to petition the government
> Freedom of worship
> Freedom to bear arms

It kicked it kicked.

Does he look like me?

Pregnant women are always in Addidas sweatpants.

I play on my america xylophone
and the kids drop peach hat by aching peach hat.

But someone of that birdcage was real.

A funnel of this bedsheet cotton purple emotion

I want to lay down on.

Cabbage world food for people on the run

Who need sustenance quick and right now and for the foreseeable future.

Following the loose protein, the hype of skin color

Lovely cousin strands.

It's as if she has already apologized to both my parents.

Like a sloppy Hansel and Gretel. Their hands dripping fruit juice.

They've already said. I'm sorry. We're sorry.

The Tip of the Angel

Represents my effort to embrace the populace

Bright green as the necklace of leaves hung outside my window.

As I will have to leave this place. And I'm not in love.

And I have no second document.

Are not the noodling dog, the jocky tiger,

the pink sleeved girl parts of our angel?

That fine-browed man who will bring down tablets from the mountain.

This is what it says. He is gesturing toward your body.

Your obvious lack of love.

Why else would you pack 20 people (I counted them) in one house?

It's what we could afford.

And I was happy to see my family.

My many-gold-rings family.

My poem which is contemporaneous with my family

Is a sturdy, big nosed child.

Who asks questions we don't like.

Asaan ka mahal ko mio?

Maybe she'll grow into her nose the family wonders glumly

Getting Used to It

She brightens at the evidence. Like a strong appliance.

You can make it hot.

Grown ass people having tantrums.

I'm unbought, unheated. Like a perfectly square morsel of lasagna.

A wrathful rubics cube.

To realize, I wish to ridicule people interested in martial arts.

That I'm not getting better.

My uncle would prank call my father, "Immigration!"

He'd crow. And my father would fall to silence.

No matter the heavy accent.

No matter the voice he'd known unto boredom.

One wing swigging out to its brother on the other bird.

I measured this silence when I was a girl.

The quality of the joke and how it rested

on the bad stomach of a tensile citizenry.

The joke was that, in an instant,

We Lost Everything.

It is important to remember who would laugh first—

the perpetrator/uncle/jokester or the assailed/father/feather.

Or, maybe, it isn't.

Maybe what you should know is that

they told this joke over and over and ever.

My uncle crowed. My father disbelieved. We lost everything.

And then, the svelte, sweet brier laughter.

Your Daddy's Rich,
Your Mama's Good Looking

Who will comfort me and my beer battered novels?
Needling in the tall grass next to the good looking colt.
Who's me. Who can be me. When I've given up.

A stranger colt.
Unskilled. Unspoken for.

My breaking plates all over the place.
And I can feel like I could be capable of you but I want to believe
I enter something holy. That I would bow my head.
That I would enter a life I don't have to earn.

Power in Numbers

You don't protect yourself.

I went to the city to protect

the softboiled neighborhood of us.

An anorak self.

Its light pours in.

It is not its signal.

Resolute as in aided not.

I am aggrieved, uninspired.

and writing my signature.

I'm holding up the sword

just to be closer to the sword.

Haka

Let go. Let me take it.

The ranunculus pea pod of your shaking

on the stem of your own velcro doing.

Braided doll. Howling insouciant.

The patient says she is currently not living with her husband and
drinks water from a cistern on and off. She is also a large smoker—
smoking, until recently, three packs per day. She drinks a six pack on
the weekends.

The tunnels had her.

Monday (3:00 pm – 5:00 pm) Tuesday (9:00 am – 12:30 pm).

Dusty sari sari stores with plastic toys,

Formaldehyde spices and styrofoam containers of excited meat

The patient was spotted in Ephesus, Sardis and Laodicea.

Debt is a number.

Am I not grieved with those that rise up? I hate them perfect hatred.

Loopholes too spacious.

The patient is a 14 yr old female with 5 to 6 month history L knee pain. 2 degree Tennis accident with twisting mechanism.

Put thou my tears in thy bottle.

Our girl is dead.

Die as you will die

They make a big to-do out of her. Then they go have affairs and crap.

As there no is other way to hold onto your linen

As if it is mine and it is dirty and I can wash it by hand.

Haka

Goodbye arctic, goodbye dreamstate. I who never knew you.
I who knew you since the day I was struck like a flint on the earth.
I mix several colors to arrive at a shade.
To box you to death.

O big belly.
Delicious char. I'm through with you.
I listen for your patent leather footsteps gleaming down the aisle.

I raise my hand for your teacher. I'm good. I'm *so* good.
Raising your hand against me in public. Making a run for it.
Styling my own appearance and joshing about.

Hymn

She throws lake water on the brown flank.

Opening timex eyes.

I pinched the mosquito. And it fell apart. Just carbon fizz.

My feelings splash away outside of me. Toddler and tissue delight.

A moth of generous proportions

Making pawprints on the fogged up vehicles.

O come to the church in the wildwood.

Me with matted blue fur.

O come to the church in the dale.

Decked in lapis lazuli, I call my x boyfriends

Flocking to them anyway.

I flock exclusively.

To be unheld and unknown.

Floored by yourself

every single time.

What I Saw

And I thought all the hunks of peaches of my

life were coming together. To hold

in my hand. And have. And eat. And

I saw a family. *Veo una familia. Isang pamilya.*

A tree. An urban sleeping, soft

family on the train. Enfolded and the husband his

arms were around the wife and the wife her

arms were around the child. Tender dips in Spanish

moss across the terrain of loving some other

foreign filament. Fishtail of when I'm stiller.

Deploying identity. I saw

a family. I saw a family. I saw a family.

She said. He said. It's possible to

hurt it to my april cove.

I believe both of them and see

them translucent. To delicate to breaking

and staying together. A human invention

to believe. Détente.

Among these trees you know we pitch

together. Crouching ever closer.

Orchard together. I saw

a family. A family like a farm. That decides.

Like a field. On its own.

Grazing and growing and grass.

I saw a family. I saw a family.

Rapprochement

The art of war teaches us to rely not on the chance of the enemy not attacking but rather on the fact that we have made our position unassailable.

—*Sun Tzu*

My father called me a chink
so I'd know how to receive it.
So I wouldn't be surprised.

Therefore the good soldier will be terrible in his onset and prompt in his decision.

In the wall, I bricked up my secret.
So it would gush forth. I did this for effect.
So you would know me.

On the day of battle your soldiers might weep bedewing their garments.

But it grew like a bullet loving its flowerstain.
It happened nonetheless.

But let them at once be brought to bay.

Because you are simply my medic watching me.
I'm a poem someone else wrote for me.
All of the characters "beautiful and flawed."

When we are near, we must make the enemy believe we are far.

My sister said, you can forget our way of life?
I said yes and was annoyed. She ran away and I was desperate for her.
I was screaming into the mindspeaker.

When far away, we must make him believe we are near.

I said, Christine, christine, christine.

Notes

"Immigration": *Mahal ko, bakit hindi ka maka tulog* translated from the Tagalog means My love, why can't you sleep.

"I need you to understand": Some lines are taken from Emmanuel Ghent's essay "Masochism, Submission, Surrender: Masochism as a Perversion of Surrender."

"Rapprochement": The italicized lines are from *The Art of War* by Sun Tzu.

About the Author

Sarah Gambito is the author of a previous poetry collection, *Matadora*. Her poems have appeared or are forthcoming in *Antioch Review, Denver Quarterly, Fence, Field, Iowa Review, New Republic, Quarterly West* and other journals. She holds degrees from the University of Virginia and the Creative Writing Program at Brown University. She is co-founder of Kundiman, a non-profit organization that promotes Asian American poetry, and is Assistant Professor and Director of Creative Writing at Fordham University. She lives in New York City.